98

RAIL 6 PORTFOLIOS

The Cromptons

Compiled by
Colin J Marsden

Copyright © Jane's Publishing Company Limited 1986

First published in the United Kingdom in 1986 by
Jane's Publishing Company Limited
238 City Road, London EC1V 2PU

ISBN 0 7106 0364 9

Printed in the United Kingdom by
Netherwood Dalton & Co Ltd

JANE'S

Cover illustrations

Front: During the early 1980s Class 33s became the regular motive
power for Exeter-Paignton, Plymouth-Exeter, and Plymouth-
Paignton stopping services. On 5 July 1984 No 33005 heads away
from Aller Junction, west of Newton Abbot, with the 1632
Plymouth-Paignton. *(Colin J Marsden)*
Mamiya 645   1000S 80mm Sekor   Ektachrome 200   1/1000, f5.6

Back: Crompton line-up at Hither Green depot on 23 August 1969,
with Nos D6562, D6504, D6568 and D6567 taking a weekend
breather. *(Colin Ding)*
Rolleiflex   80mm Planar   Agfa Professional   1/125, f11

Right: Class 33/0 No 33042 dozes under the splendid LBSCR roof at
Brighton station on 29 September 1984 after arriving with an 'Adex'
from Holyhead. The 33 had operated the train from Mitre Bridge
Junction. *(Michael J Collins)*
Olympus OM1   50mm Zuiko   Kodachrome 64   1/60, f6.3

Introduction

The BRCW Type 3s, better known as the Class 33s, were introduced as a direct result of the 1955 Modernisation Plan, which called for the eventual replacement of steam traction with up-to-date diesel and electric types. Orders were placed during the mid-1950s and deliveries of the BRCW-built Type 3s fitted with Crompton-Parkinson electrical equipment — from where the nickname 'Crompton' originated — commenced at the end of 1959, the first machine, No D6500, commencing test and trial running in the spring of 1960. By the time the first locomotive had entered traffic a total of 98 had been ordered. The final twelve examples were built to the narrow 'Hastings' profile, 7 inches slimmer than the other 86. These proved very costly to produce, considerably exceeding the original tender price. Due to production problems, mainly involving the 'slim' variant, the delivery period was far longer than initially planned, with the last machine not handed over until May 1962.

All locomotives were initially allocated to the South Eastern Division but by 1964 their operating area had been considerably enlarged, with their presence recorded all over the SR and also in a number of 'foreign' areas including Exeter, York and Birmingham.

Enthusiast reception for Cromptons in the early 1960s was at best indifferent, mostly they were despised because of their rapid displacement of steam. However new 'strains' of railway enthusiasts have developed and the following for diesels seems to be at an all-time high, with an almost fanatical devotion to some classes, including the Class 33s.

The Class 33 fleet in 1985 numbered 94, divided into three sub-classes: 33/0 (33001-035/037-040/042-065), 33/1 (33101-119), 33/2 (33201-212). All can be found operating throughout the SR as well as on a number of LMR and WR duties.

It is expected that the Cromptons will remain in traffic for many years to come, probably breaking new operating ground. This book tries to give an insight into the Class 33 story and shows Cromptons at work and rest in a variety of locations and liveries. It is hoped that readers will enjoy browsing through this volume and viewing these remarkable, versatile machines and that they receive as much pleasure from it as it gave me in the compilation.

I would like to express my thanks to the many photographers who have assisted me with material. A special thank you must also go to Mrs J Marsden for typing and secretarial work.

COLIN J MARSDEN
Worcester Park
November 1985

Below. The BRCW Type 3s commenced operation on the SR's South Eastern Division from January 1960, first operating training and trial specials on the Kent main lines. No D6502 is illustrated at Folkestone Junction carriage sidings with empty 'blood and custard' liveried Mk I stock on 5 June 1960. This locomotive was involved in a serious collision at Itchingfield Junction, near Christ's Hospital, on 5 March 1964 and subsequently withdrawn. *(Rodney A Lissenden) Agfa Silette Agfa CT18*

When introduced, the BRCW Type 3s were all allocated to Hither Green depot in South East London, but by July 1962 the Western Section were in need of diesel traction mainly to obviate the need to double-head selected oil and freight trains in the Eastleigh and Southampton areas. To overcome this problem 12 members of the fleet were allocated to Eastleigh from 7 July 1962. No D6509 is seen near Sway on 10 September 1966 with a splendid loose-coupled freight train bound for Eastleigh. *(Michael Mensing)*
Nikkorex F 50mm Nikkor Agfa CT18 1/500, f3.2

Above. To provide 'modern' motive power for the restricted clearances on the Hastings route south of Tonbridge, the final twelve BRCW Type 3s were built to the 8ft 8in loading gauge as opposed to the conventional 9ft 3in of the remaining 86. The work involved in slimming these locomotives was considerable, with a number of internal fittings having to be re-designed. From their outward appearance the 'slimline' machines are readily identifiable as their body sides continue straight upwards from the frame width; revision was also made to the air intakes at cantrail height. No D6595 (now No 33210) stands at Eastleigh shed in company with straight electric No E5018 on 24 January 1963. In this view the locomotive's No 1 end is on the right. *(Les Elsey)*
Agfa Silette 50mm Color Solinar
Agfa CT18 1/60, f8

Right. From the summer of 1963 the machines commenced operation on selected Waterloo-Bournemouth, West of England and some cross-country diagrams, replacing steam trac-tion earlier than originally planned. The Type 3s not fitted with steam heating were precluded from operating passenger services in the winter months and returned to freight duties between October and April until suitable electrically heated stock could be made available. No D6560 with a rake of green-liveried MkIs is seen near Salisbury on 3 August 1964 with the 11.10 am Plymouth-Brighton.
(Michael Mensing)
Nikkorex F 50mm Nikkor Agfa CT18
1/1000, f2.5

Above. The first regular freight diagrams on the Western Section that fell to BRCW Type 3 haulage were seven daily Fawley oil duties during 1962, the Type 3s usually operating between the South Coast terminal and Didcot, Southall or Feltham. With a lengthy train of four-wheeled Esso wagons, No D6549 approaches Southampton Central on 12 September 1964 with a train bound for Feltham.

(Gavin Morrison)
Zeiss Contaflex   Tessar   Agfa CT18

Right. In the early 1960s oil traffic to and from Fawley considerably increased, with petro-chemical products going to virtually all parts of the country, supplying railway installations and private transfer terminals. On a bright 1

April 1965 No D6536 double-heads with sister locomotive No D6545 past Allbrook, north of Eastleigh, with the daily Bromford Bridge-Fawley service. The BRCW Type 3s were fitted from new with the blue star electro-pneumatic multiple control facility enabling one driver to control up to three machines.

(Les Elsey)
Agfa Silette   Agfa CT18   1/500, f5.6

Above and right. In the early 1960s a number of Western, Eastern and London Midland Region crews were trained in BRCW Type 3 operation. This naturally widened the locomotives' operating potential and saved the need to change engines on inter-regional diagrams. Two of the Type 3s most famous 'foreign' activities are illustrated on this spread. The plate above shows the Bromford Bridge-Fawley empty oil train at Bentley Crossing, near Knowle & Dorridge, during 1965 headed by Nos D6544 and D6534. *(Michael Mensing)*
Nikkorex F 50mm Nikkor Agfa CT18 1/500, f3.2

The plate opposite depicts the Cliffe-Uddingston powdered cement train which commenced operation in December 1961, taking the SR Type 3s to York on a daily basis. Indeed, it was not uncommon for the SR traction to operate considerably further north. At first the train was always double-headed, but after a short period one machine was found adequate to haul the train. In April 1962 the train is seen at Marholm on the ECML with locomotives Nos D6577 and D6562 providing the power. *(Colin Ding)*
Microcord High Speed Ektachrome 1/300, f8

BEWARE
OF
TRAINS.

Left. During the summer of 1962 some South Western section main line passenger duties were diesel-operated. One such train was the 7.20 am Eastleigh-Waterloo which is seen here about to depart on its 73½-mile journey to the capital in July 1962, headed by No D6546. The passenger accommodation is formed of a splendid rake of Bulleid-designed stock. The difference between SR and BR green livery is clearly visible in this illustration. *(Les Elsey)*
Agfa Silette 50mm Color Solinar
Perutz C18 1/125, f8

Left. The task of conveying passengers and guests between the capital and the dock complex at Southampton has been undertaken by the railway for many years. In the period when the railway took pride in these prestigious trains immaculate stock and often ex-works locomotives were provided, but alas today any available locomotive is diagrammed with often far-from-pristine stock. On 2 July 1962 No D6510 was given the job of taking guests back to London after visiting the *Northern Star* at Southampton; the passenger accommodation was entirely Pullman with an ex-LMS full brake at the front. The illustration of this superb train was taken near Swaythling.
(Les Elsey)
Agfa Silette 50mm Color Solinar
Perutz C18 1/125, f8

BRCW Type 3 in original condition. The main body is painted in BR locomotive green, relieved by the 3in off-white band mid-way up the body. The cab and door window surrounds are also finished in the same light colour, the roof was in mid-grey, while the underframe was black. The bufferbeam was painted in signal red and carried air control, main reservoir, vacuum, brake pipe and electric train-heat jumpers; there were also sockets for the multiple-control equipment. No D6536 is illustrated from the No 1 (radiator) end at Brighton. The locomotive was at Brighton to assist drawing office staff in the future fitting of AWS equipment. *(Colin Boocock)*
Voigtlander Vito IIa 50mm Color Skopar Agfa CT18

11

Left. In conjunction with the electrification and modernisation of the Waterloo-Bournemouth line a number of major track possessions took place in 1965/66, necessitating major diversions from booked routes. When the section of line between Pirbright Junction and Winchester Junction was blocked, trains were diverted via Aldershot, Alton and the mid-Hants 'over the Alps' line. The 1.30 pm Waterloo-Bournemouth headed by No D6540 is seen near Bentley on 1 May 1966 formed of a grand array of Bulleid stock. *(T B Owen)*
Leica M2 50mm Summicron
Kodachrome II

Above. All services west of Pirbright Junction had to be loco-operated until early January 1967 when the 'live rail' was switched on for public services as far as Basingstoke; the 'switch-on' through to Bournemouth followed a few weeks later, but regular services did not commence until 10 July 1967 due to late delivery of rolling stock and operating problems. During 1966 and early 1967 the Waterloo-Basingstoke duties were a mixture of steam and diesel formations. The 5.09 pm Waterloo-Basingstoke of 17 August 1966 is seen departing from Woking and passing Woking Junction with No D6570 in charge of a mixture of BR Mk I and SR main line and suburban vehicles. *(T B Owen)*
Leica M2 50mm Summicron
Kodachrome II 1/400, f2.6

13

Below. In the mid-1960s the British Railways Board decided that staff working on or near the track should have as much advance warning as possible of trains approaching. It was therefore decided to apply small yellow warning panels on the front of locomotives as they received classified attention. In near 'ex-shops' condition No D6554 heads a down freight near Grateley on 22 January 1967. This locomotive, later to become No 33036, was involved in a collision at Mottingham on 10 October 1977 which regretfully led to its withdrawal and cutting up at Slade Green. *(T B Owen)*
Leica M2   50mm Summicron
Kodachrome II

Right. During the transition period from steam to diesel/electric traction, the SR had to dispose of well over 1000 steam locomotives. This led to the operation of many specials hauling 'dead' steam locomotives to storage, disposal or scrapping locations. On 16 October 1966 Type 3 No D6525 was entrusted with one of these specials, and is seen near Witley with two BR Standard locomotives and a brake van. The Type 3 was later rebuilt into one of the push-pull members of Class 33/1, No 33109.
(T B Owen)
Leica M2   90mm Summicron
Kodachrome II

Left. The BRCW or Crompton Type 3s have carried a number of different liveries over the years. As already mentioned, when built the machines were in all-over green; in mid-1962 No D6530 was the first locomotive to be given a small yellow warning panel by Eastleigh and this was later adopted as standard for all locomotives. However No D6530 remained identifiable for many years as the yellow panel had rounded corners at the top whereas others had squared-off top corners. The locomotive's No 2 end is nearest to the camera in this illustration taken at Eastleigh on 28 August 1962. *(Les Elsey)*
Agfa Silette
50mm Color Solinar
Perutz C18   1/125, f6.3

Left. After it became obvious that the yellow panels were assisting 'on-line' safety, full yellow ends were decided upon as the norm for the future. Many thought that this spoilt the Cromptons' aesthetic appearance with the white body band and window surrounds now being lost. The full yellow end treatment is displayed on No 6582, devoid of its 'D' prefix, at Crewe Works on 26 January 1969. It was photographed during the short period that the class visited the works for classified attention. *(John Glover)*
Praktica Nova
50mm Tessar   Agfa CT18

Right. The livery transition period from green to blue lasted from 1966 to 1971, when the final machines passed through Eastleigh Works and emerged in rail blue. During the late 1960s the BRCW Type 3s became Class 33 under the BR numerical classification system. Standard machines were designated Class 33/0; those modified for 'push-pull' operation 33/1, and the narrow-bodied 'slimline' locomotives Class 33/2. Green, full yellow end-liveried No D6566 leads rail blue No D6588 at Gillingham with the 0850 Brighton-Exeter train of 29 August 1970. This South Coast-West Country through train was usually double-headed in summer months due to the loading of up to 10 or 12 bogies being too heavy for a single Class 33.
(Hugh Ballantyne)
Voigtlander CLR   50mm Skopar
Agfa CT18   1/250, f8

Right. In conjunction with the Waterloo-Bournemouth electrification in 1966/67, 19 standard Class 33/0s were modified with push-pull equipment, enabling them to operate at the remote ends of post-1951 EMU and TC stock. The installation of the equipment was effected at Eastleigh Works and some people thought it cluttered the front-end appearance of the machines. As the locomotives emerged from conversion work they appeared in rail blue livery with full yellow ends, except the first conversion, No D6580, which entered traffic in green with small yellow warning panels. One of the converted examples, No D6527, approaches Totton on 18 June 1967 with a Bournemouth-Waterloo semi-fast service.
(Les Elsey)
Agfa Silette
50mm Color Solinar
Agfa CT18   1/500, f5.6

The 19 Eastleigh-allocated push-pull Class 33/1s are usually employed on duties with TC or unit formations. The additional items installed during modification included buck-eye couplers, rubbing plates, Oleo retractable buffers, waist-high air connections and MU jumper cables. This view clearly shows the additional equipment as fitted to No 33119 on the No 2 end. The locomotive was captured on film at Clapham Junction on 21 September 1978 while working the 0800 Manchester Piccadilly-Windsor & Eaton Riverside day excursion, which the Class 33/1 operated forward from Mitre Bridge Junction.

(Colin J Marsden)
Pentax KM 55mm Takumar
Kodachrome 64 1/250, f8

There are few London stations where one can photograph such a clear panoramic view of a train departing as at Waterloo, when standing on the stairway of a nearby block of flats! In this photograph taken on 26 April 1984 the area from platform 3 (on far right) to platform 15 (on the left) can be seen. Departing from platform 8 is the 1700 Waterloo-Yeovil Junction/Eastleigh headed by No 33113. This service is quite unusual as it is formed of a Class 33/1 and Class 491 4TC unit with two Class 423 (4VEPs) on the rear, all of which are under the control of the driver of the Class 33/1, who has a total of 3550hp at his disposal.

When this train arrives at Basingstoke the Class 33 and 4TC are detached, carrying on to Yeovil Junction, while another driver takes the rear VEP portion on to Eastleigh.
(Ken Harris)
Pentax SP1000   55mm Takumar
Kodachrome 25   1/250, f4

Left. Four Eastleigh-allocated Class 33/1s are required each day to operate the hourly service between Bournemouth and Weymouth, which is formed of the TC portion off the fast services from Waterloo. The Class 33/1s haul these trains in the down direction and propel the unit stock, under the control of the driver in the TC, on the up trip. The distance between Bournemouth and Weymouth is 34¾ miles and the train takes 60 minutes to make the journey with eight intermediate stops. Pulling out of the south-western portal of Bincombe Tunnel on 27 May 1978 is the 1330 service from Waterloo led by Crompton No 33116. (*John Medley*)
Canon TL6   50mm Canon
Kodachrome 25   1/500, f2.5

Right. One of the daily spectacles for holidaymakers in Weymouth during the summer months is the arrival/departure of the Channel Islands boat train which operates between Waterloo and Weymouth Quay. For the duration of the 1985 summer the service departed from Waterloo at 0940, usually behind a Class 73, and arrived at Bournemouth at 1130, where the electro-diesel would be replaced by a Class 33/1 for the remainder of the journey. Immediately before Weymouth station the train veers off at Weymouth Junction, where a warning bell/light unit is attached. The train then traverses the streets of the town to arrive at the Quay station at 1247. Between Weymouth Junction and the Quay the train only travels at walking pace and is usually escorted by shunting staff on foot and a police car making sure that the road ahead is clear. Class 33/1 No 33115 makes slow headway for the Quay on 5 September 1984 with the down working. (*Brian Morrison*)
Nikon FE   Nikkor 50mm
Kodachrome 64   1/500, f4.5

Above. 13·26 miles from Waterloo lays Hampton Court Junction, where the Hampton Court and Guildford via Cobham branches diverge. Racing towards the capital under the down Hampton Court line flyover, No 33015 leads the 0737 Exeter-Waterloo of 4 April 1980, a few weeks prior to the take-over of the SR West of England route by Class 50s. The train is formed of Mk IIb stock together with a Mk I refreshment vehicle. This locomotive is one of 24 Class 33s fitted with 3-piece miniature snowploughs suitable for ploughing small snow accumulations. *(Colin J Marsden)*
Pentax KM   55mm Takumar
Kodachrome 64   1/500, f4

Right. Since the revision of the Waterloo-Salisbury-Exeter route timetable in 1980 additional 'short-haul' services between Waterloo and Salisbury have been operated at alternate hours to the two-hourly Exeter trains. The 1010 and 1210 departures from Waterloo have been formed of Class 33/1s and TC stock, while the 1410 is still operated with loco-hauled stock. The 1010 departure from Waterloo is seen passing Weybridge on 9 July 1985 headed by Class 33/1 No 33103, trailing TC units 419 and 430. *(Colin J Marsden)*
Nikon FM2   Nikkor 85mm   Kodachrome 64
1/500, f4

The London Division of the Western section sees little freight traffic today except for the occasional engineers' departmental special and the almost daily coal traffic to Chessington and Tolworth. Until 1979 an infrequent duty was the 0740 Fawley-Waddon Marsh power station oil train which operated on an 'as required' basis. The train was photographed approaching Wimbledon West yard on 22 September 1978 headed by push-pull No 33118. When this train operated it ran from Fawley to Wimbledon West Yard, where it ran round before taking the single Wimbledon-West Croydon line to Waddon Marsh.
(Colin J Marsden)
Pentax KM   55mm Takumar
Kodachrome 64   1/500, f4

The two coal distribution depots on the suburban Chessington branch, located at Tolworth and Chessington South, still receive one booked train Monday-Friday each week. This is only a shadow of the service operated during the 1970s, when five trains per day were the norm. Usually the Class 73 or 74 electro-diesels were entrusted with these duties but occasionally the more powerful (in diesel terms) Class 33s were used. This view taken on 22 September 1978 shows the 1125 Wimbledon West Yard-Chessington headed by No 33028 shunting in the sidings at Chessington South. The coal brought to these two South London terminals was mined in South Wales and transferred to the SR via Acton Yard.

(Colin J Marsden)
Pentax KM   55mm Takumar
Kodachrome 64   1/250, f5.6

Left. Until May 1985 all SR services were booked to carry a two-character headcode but some staff decided that two white blanks would suffice as frontal indication. From May 1985 no two-character headcodes have been allocated to freight trains except for engineering specials where the codes assist staff in identifying individual trains. No 33106 slowly departs from Southampton on the down main line on 16 August 1983 at the head of a Fawley oil duty. Note the two Railfreight vans in the formation acting as barrier vehicles on a loaded train. *(Ken Harris)*
Pentax SP1000 80mm Zeiss
Kodachrome 25 1/250, f4

Above. During weekend engineering possessions a large amount of spent ballast is dug and usually loaded into wagons and later despatched to the SR spoil tip located at Farnham, this operation taking a number of locomotive-hauled trains on to the Pirbright Junction-Alton line, which would otherwise be just another branch of the great EMU tree. With dark storm clouds giving a dramatic skyline, Class 33/0 No 33014 pulls out of Farnham yard onto the up line with an empty trip freight bound for Guildford on 28 May 1980. *(Andrew French)*
Pentax KM 55mm Takumar
Kodachrome 64 1/500, f4

27

Left. Today, with fewer people using solid fuel for domestic heating, the number of local coal trains on the SR can now almost be counted on one hand. One such train that has now long ceased to run was the twice-weekly Basingstoke-Farnborough coal, always formed of 16·5 ton capacity MCV wagons, as these were more suitable for discharging at Farnborough than conventional coal hoppers. Class 33/1 No 33104 approaches Hook on 10 May 1978 with the Farnborough-bound duty. This locomotive was involved in a serious collision near Micheldever on 26 January 1985 and was subsequently withdrawn. *(Colin J Marsden)*
Pentax KM 55mm
Takumar Kodachrome 64
1/500, f4.5

Right. With the BR decision to withdraw its parcels collection and delivery service from the early 1980s, the numbers of NPCCS vehicles and trains were considerably reduced. The daily departures from London to Southampton Docks and Bournemouth were lost, as were a number of inter-regional workings. On 5 September 1979, when the photographer was in position awaiting the Mountbatten funeral train, Class 33/0 No 33021 was captured on film passing Wallers Ash, between Micheldever and Winchester, heading a Basingstoke-Southampton Western Dock parcels duty. The Wallers Ash passenger loops, visible in the distance, have since been considerably shortened and the main line completely realigned. *(Colin J Marsden)*
Pentax KM 55mm Takumar Kodachrome 64 1/500, f4

Earl Mountbatten of Burma

Above. Following the tragic death of Lord Louis Mountbatten in Ireland on 27 August 1979, a full ceremonial funeral was held at Westminster Abbey on 5 September. After the service and a procession through the streets of London the coffin was loaded onto a special train at Waterloo and taken to Romsey for burial near the late Earl's residence at Broadlands. The special train also conveyed the complete British Royal Family and a number of heads of state from many foreign countries. After the sudden death of Earl Mountbatten and the decision to operate a funeral train, the SR had hastily to arrange stock and motive power. Class 33s Nos 33027 and 33056 were the latest 'ex-works' machines so these were selected and prepared by Stewarts Lane. The upper plate shows the funeral train headed by that pair near Basingstoke. Note the Royal headlight on the front and the Royal Train escort coach behind the locomotives. A year after the funeral the BRB decided to name the two funeral train engines in memory of Earl Mountbatten, No 33027 becoming *Earl Mountbatten of Burma* and No 33056 *The Burma Star*. The nameplate and family crest carried by No 33027 are inset left. *(Above: Andrew French)*
Pentax KM 135mm Takumar
Kodachrome 64 1/250, f6
(Inset: Hugh Ballantyne)
Leica M4-2 Summicron 50mm
Kodachrome 25 1/30, f2.8

Right. The external appearance of the named Class 33s is usually kept respectable. No 33027 *Earl Mountbatten of Burma*, complete with grey cab roof and yellow snowploughs, heads the 1055 Teesport-Salfords oil train past the splendid semaphore signals at Junction Road Junction near Upper Holloway on the North London route on 21 July 1983. The miniature snowplough should consist of three pieces but during the summer months the centre section is removed to assist in clearances, when staff are required to go between locomotives and stock for coupling purposes. *(Hugh Dady)*
Nikkormat FT2 50mm Nikkor
Kodachrome 64 1/500, f4

Left. A sizeable amount of freight traffic traverses the West London Extension Railway between Latchmere Junction and Willesden each day. The majority of inter-regional traffic consists of trains to/from the dock complex at Dover, but several oil, coal and departmental trains are to be found. With LRT electrified tracks feeding Kensington Olympia and Lillie Bridge depot in the foreground, Class 33/0 No 33057 passes between Kensington and West Brompton on 15 April 1980 with an MCV coal train bound for Norwood Yard. *(Colin Whitbread)*
Nikon FM 50mm Nikkor Ektachrome 64 1/500, f4.5

Left. Crompton No 33052 was twinned with the railway town of Ashford, Kent on 15 May 1980 when it was given the name *Ashford* in a ceremony performed by the then Mayor of the town, Councillor H Apps. The machine is seen approaching Factory Junction in South London while heading the 0730 Congleton-Dover Priory excursion of 30 June 1980. The train was running over 90 minutes late at this location because of a hot box on one of the coaches which necessitated its removal. In the background, behind the first coach of the train, Stewarts Lane electric depot can be seen. *(Colin Whitbread)*
Olympus OM1 50mm Zuiko Ektachrome 64 1/250, f5.6

Hither Green was the home of the 12 slimline Class 33/2s until its closure in late 1985, when the complete allocation was transferred to Stewarts Lane. Diagrams specifically requiring the Hastings gauge machines are now few, one of those remaining being the Mountfield-Northfleet gypsum train. Class 33/2 No 33202 approaches Culvert Road Junction off the West London Extension Railway on 5 July 1984 with the infrequent Tavistock Junction-Dover export china clay train formed of Polybulk wagons. *(Ken Harris)*
Yashica TL Electro X 50mm Yashinon
Kodachrome 25 1/250, f3.5

Left. In recent years, as the Class 33s have gained something of a cult following, the 12 narrow-bodied machines have become affectionately known as 'Slim Jims' and their operation on passenger trains followed by an ardent band of enthusiasts. The Class 33/2s are unique amongst the breed as they are fitted with slow speed control (SSC) equipment for MGR purposes, although this equipment is seldom used except on the Northfleet circuit. Passengers aboard a Northampton-Margate excursion on 13 May 1976 were lucky enough to be hauled forward from Mitre Bridge Junc-tion by 'Slim Jim' No 33203, which was captured on film near Shortlands. *(R C Riley) Canon FTQL 50mm Canon Kodachrome 25 1/250, f4*

Above. The North-South inter-regional services to/from Bournemouth/Poole and Weymouth mostly traverse the LSWR main line as far as Basingstoke and then take the ex-GWR route to Reading, where trains either run-round or are provided with a fresh loco-motive for their journey to Oxford, Birming-ham and the North. Class 47s are usually rostered for these turns but for several days early in May 1985 a 'Slim Jim' Class 33/2 No 33208 was used on the portions south of Reading. The 0650 Liverpool Lime Street-Poole of 6 May 1985 is seen passing the site of the junction of the former GWR goods line to Reading Central at Southcote Junction. The 'window hangers' in the front coach probably indicate a number of Class 33 haulage 'freaks' were aboard!
(Ken Harris) Yashica TL Electro X 80mm Zeiss Kodachrome 25 1/500, f2.8

Left. From the demise of the Class 42 'Warship' locomotives in 1971 until May 1980 the Class 33s reigned supreme on the Waterloo-Salisbury-Exeter route; train consists were normally restricted to eight coaches in winter months when electric train heating was required, but in the high season 9-car formations of usually Mk I stock were provided. Departing from the eastern portal of Fisherton Tunnel and passing Salisbury Tunnel Junction, immaculate EH-allocated No 33005 heads the 1210 Salisbury-Waterloo on 27 August 1983.
(Michael Mensing).
Bronica S2A   75mm Nikkor
Afgachrome R100S
1/1000, f4.7

Right. On Fridays and Saturdays a through service between Brighton and the West of England operates. For the duration of the 1985 timetable the Friday service left Brighton at 1114 arriving in Penzance at 1859, while the Saturday train departed two hours earlier, arriving in the Cornish terminal at 1708. These cross-country services are Crompton-operated as far as Exeter, where a Class 50 usually takes over for the remainder of the journey. This well-executed through-the-trees shot of the Brighton-Penzance train was taken at Tisbury on 10 November 1984 and shows No 33054 complete with snowploughs.
(John Vaughan)
Nikon FG20
50mm Nikkor
Kodachrome 64   1/500, f4

Above. Throughout 1984 and early 1985 the area around Exeter saw considerable change, with the beautiful semaphore signals replaced by the latest multi-aspect colour light types and significant track rationalisation carried out. This included the removal of the centre roads at Exeter St Davids and Central stations and the introduction of bi-directional running. In happier days when semaphores still prevailed, and with a centre road still present,

Class 33/0 No 33028 pulls the 1010 Exeter-Waterloo up the bank from Exeter St Davids into Exeter Central. 17 July 1976.
(John Medley)
Canon TL6   50mm Canon   Kodachrome 25 1/250 f3.5
Right. On summer Saturdays, when additional services between Waterloo-Salisbury and Exeter are operated, Class 33s are diagrammed, as little spare capacity exists in the Class

50 rosters and indeed any spare machines are required for WR operation. The 0840 (SO) Waterloo-Exeter of 29 April 1984, headed by Hither Green-allocated No 33051, departs from the short Blackboy Tunnel, near Exmouth Junction, and approaches St James Park Halt, just 1¼ miles before journey's end.
(David Mitchell)
Pentax 6 × 7   105mm Takumar Agfachrome R100S   1/500, f6.3

Right. From 1980, when spare capacity prevailed in Class 33 diagrams, some West of England 'local' duties were taken over by the class. These included the Exeter-Barnstaple and Exeter-Paignton services and in most cases the Cromptons replaced life-expired Class 25s which had been re-allocated away to the LMR or withdrawn. Departing from Kings Nympton (formerly South Moulton Road) No 33052 *Ashford* hauls the 1715 Exeter-Barnstaple on 18 August 1984. As these WR duties are not allocated two position headcodes two white blanks have to suffice.
(Rodney A Lissenden)
Pentax 6 × 7
300mm Takumar
Agfa CT18   1/250, f4

Opposite. Usually the Exeter-Barnstaple branch is operated by Class 118 DMMUs, but a couple of trains per day that operate as a through service to Paignton are loco-operated and are usually formed of five Mk I coaches. Under stormy skies No 33017 passes Yeoford on 2 October 1984 with the 1500 Exeter-Barnstaple. On its return from the North Devon coast this service operated through to Paignton.
(Colin J Marsden)
Nikon FM2   50mm Nikkor
Kodachrome 64
1/1000, f3.5

Left. One of the infrequent Paignton-Exeter stopping services, the 1830 from Paignton, is seen at Hollicombe, near Torquay, on 10 June 1985, headed by No 33053. It is usual practice for Class 33s used on West of England duties to arrive either on services from Bristol or on one-way freight diagrams from Westbury. Whilst away from the SR the Cromptons receive only the minimum of repair and often return to the Southern in a far from healthy state. (*Ian Gould*)

Pentax 6 × 7   200mm Takumar
Ektachrome 200   1/250, f11

Above. One of the first regular Class 33 diagrams into the West Country was the Fawley-Plymouth oil tanks, taking diesel fuel to Laira depot. This diagram commenced with Class 33s during the mid-1970s and usually operated on a Thursday only, arriving in the West around 0730 and returning at around mid-day. The train was routed from Fawley via Eastleigh, Salisbury and Westbury to join the WR main line, returning via the reverse route. On occasions if this service had a particularly heavy loading, it was double-headed in the 'down' direction between Newton Abbot and Plymouth over the arduous Devon banks. No 33011 approaches Aller Junction in September 1977 with the 'up' working. (*David C Rogers*)
Pentax SP1000   55mm Takumar
Kodachrome II   1/250, f3.8

43

Nocturnal 1. To many casual observers the railway is only seen during the day time, but some of the most interesting workings occur during the night hours. Of course photography, particularly in colour, is not easy in these conditions but with a little preparation and some thought, very pleasing and sometimes quite dramatic results can be obtained. The most important element for the night photographer is a good sturdy tripod as the exposure will be long compared to that for daylight work, varying (on 64 asa film) between 2 and 60 seconds, depending on available light. Class 33/0 No 33043 stands at London Bridge on 7 January 1984 with empty vans for New Cross Gate yard, while in the background No 73006 can be seen. *(Hugh Dady)*
Nikkormat FT2   50mm Nikkor
Kodachrome 64   10 sec, f4

Nocturnal 2. The 'Night Ferry' service from London Victoria was the only train formed of Continental passenger rolling stock to operate in this country. The train linking London with Paris was usually worked by a Class 33 or 73 in Britain as far as Dover, from where stock would be loaded onto the train ferry for Dunkerque, from where the SNCF operated the train forward to Paris Gare-du-Nord. At least one BR brake vehicle was usually attached to the formation (country end) thus providing accommodation for the guard and safety equipment. From 31 October 1980 BR decided to end the 'Night Ferry' service and convey continental passengers to the Channel ports by conventional train services. The very last southbound 'Night Ferry' was headed by Class 33 No 33043, adorned with a suitable headboard which was produced by the Carriage & Wagon Department at Stewarts Lane. The train is seen awaiting departure from Victoria. *(Colin Whitbread)*
Olympus OM1   50mm Zuiko   Ektachrome 64 15 sec, f8

On 2 December 1981 Eastleigh-allocated No 33012 was released from the diesel depot following a classified exam painted in 'revised' livery. The rail blue body was retained but wrap round yellow ends were applied together with black window surrounds and a grey roof. Conventional-size numbers and logo were applied and the number was repeated centrally on the front end. After a short period the choice of livery became quite controversial, with Regional authorities disclaiming responsibility for the repaint and announcing that it was 'totally unofficial'. In late 1982 the machine was scheduled for classified works attention and emerged from Eastleigh in standard colours. Perhaps it should be regretted that depots are not given authority to modify liveries on a restricted basis, as it would certainly brighten up the diesel fleet. On 28 April 1982 No 33012 departs from Salisbury with the 1310 Portsmouth-Bristol service.
(Stephen Montgomery)
Minolta SRT101B   50mm Rokkor
Kodachrome 25   1/500, f2.8

A further revision to the standard livery policy came in 1982 when a number of Eastleigh's push-pull examples were released from the depot with white cab and door window surrounds. Although this was, of course, carried out with the best possible will, many considered this addition as messy, particularly when machines became discoloured. This revised colour scheme is displayed on No 33107, photographed in multiple with No 33030 at the head of the 1220 Exeter-Waterloo of 12 February 1983 near Wilton, west of Salisbury. Even when two Class 33s operating in multiple head a 9-car train, they cannot equal the performance of a Class 50, mainly because the Cromptons are restricted to a maximum speed of 85 mph. *(John Chalcraft)*
Mamiya 645 1000S   80mm Sekkor
Agfa R100S

Left. For some time during the 1960s and 1970s the cross-country Portsmouth-Bristol/Cardiff route had given the operating authorities cause for concern; passenger returns were encouraging but indifferent stock and motive power gave the route a bad name. At various times DEMUs, DMMUs, Class 31s and Hymeks were tried, but all to no real advantage. From May 1980 the service was completely recast with Class 33s and five or six Mk Is being used. New improved schedules were introduced and in the coming years the 'Wessex Line' trade name was applied to the route. The journey from the South Coast to Bristol passes through some beautiful scenic countryside and provides some lush photographic locations. Crompton No 33038 passes Limpley Stoke in the Avon Valley on 8 June 1984 with the 1405 Bristol Temple Meads-Portsmouth Harbour. *(John Vaughan)*
Nikon FM2 85mm Nikkor Kodachrome 64 1/500, f4.5

Below. After relinquishing the reins of the Waterloo-Exeter route, some spare capacity in Class 33 diagrams was dedicated to internal WR services. The SR Type 3s were welcomed by the WR authorities as the majority of their train crews were familiar with their operation and little re-training had to take place. In the 1984/5 timetable the few Bristol-Taunton local services were diagrammed for Class 33 power. On 29 March 1985 the 0915 service from Bristol pauses at Bridgwater headed by push-pull No 33117. It was unusual for a push-pull example to operate on WR internal services as the SR usually presses for their return due to shortages for their own commitments.
(Colin J Marsden)
Nikon FM2 50mm Nikkor Kodachrome 64 1/250, f2.4

Perhaps surprising was the decision to diagram Class 33s for selected West Wales duties from May 1982. The WR Cardiff area had responsibility for six of the class, operating them on 3-day cycle diagrams involving WR internal and Cardiff-Crewe turns. As prophesied by many railway staff and enthusiasts, the 3-day diagrams were, on occasions, considerably stretched and during the autumn of 1982 one locomotive was recorded operating from Cardiff for 14 consecutive days. The West Wales duties did break new ground for the class, taking them to Swansea, Fishguard and Milford Haven. No 33022 departs from Haverfordwest on 7 September 1983 at the head of the 0827 Milford Haven-Swansea. *(Hugh Ballantyne)*

Leica M4-2   90mm Summicron
Kodachrome 25   1/250, f2.8

A handful of Portsmouth-Bristol services are extended to Cardiff; these trains are sometimes operated by the same engine throughout, running round at Bristol Temple Meads, whilst others are re-engined, this being dependent on motive power availability at the time. The through Cardiff-Portsmouth trains take around 4 hours for the 141½-mile journey — thankfully these services are not operated under the InterCity flag! No 33026 descends Ashley Down Bank on the outskirts of Bristol on 29 May 1985 with the 0805 Cardiff-Portsmouth. *(Ian Gould)*
Pentax 6 × 7   105mm Takumar
Ektachrome 100   1/500, f5.6

From 1977 until May 1981 the Crewe-Cardiff route was mainly operated by Class 25s, but again as capacity was found in Class 33 diagrams the opportunity was taken to place these higher-powered machines on the route, the locomotives taking over from the commencement of the 1981/2 timetable in May. The Class 33 operated from the Cardiff end of the route, again in supposedly 3-day cycle diagrams, but as time has proved this has not always been the case. Whilst operating on the route maintenance is carried out either at Cardiff or Crewe Diesel Depot. Posing alongside a Class 85, Class 33 No 33006 makes ready to depart from Crewe on 18 September 1982 with the 1602 Cardiff-bound train.
(Gavin Morrison)
Pentax SP1000   Kodachrome 25

Since the Cromptons have operated the 138¾ mile Crewe-Cardiff services a number of Crewe-based drivers have been trained on the traction, thus leading to members of the class operating to many London Midland locations, including Stoke, Derby, Chester and Manchester Victoria. The operators find the SR machines extremely reliable and they are well liked by train crews and depot staff. Passing Gaer Junction, West of Newport, No 33005 makes light work of the remaining 11¾ miles on to Cardiff with the 1003 service from Crewe on 25 July 1984. *(John Medley)*
Canon TL6   50mm Canon   Kodachrome 25
1/250, f3.5

From their introduction in 1960 until mid-1985 the Class 33s have only ever been allocated to four depots. When first delivered all machines went to Hither Green but by July 1962 some were re-allocated to Eastleigh, and a year later the 12 slimline machines went to Hastings St Leonards depot. In late 1985 Stewarts Lane became home depot for the former Hither Green allocation when the latter closed for maintenance purposes. Classified depot overhauls are normally carried out at the owning depot but 'in service' running checks and fuelling can be performed by any locomotive servicing point. For example, locomotives operating on the Portsmouth-Bristol service would receive fuel and a service check at both Fratton and Bristol Bath Road but if any major defect was identified the home depot would be advised and the locomotive worked home as soon as possible. The upper plate shows HG No 33064 standing by the fuelling equipment at Fratton while the lower depicts EH No 33006 standing in the depot yard at Eastleigh in company with Classes 08 and 73. (Both: *Colin J Marsden*) *Pentax KM 55mm Takumar Kodachrome 64 Top: 1/125, f4 Bottom: 1/250, f8*

Eastleigh is now the only works within BREL to undertake repairs to Class 33s, although in the late 1960s/early 1970s Crewe undertook some intermediate overhauls during modernisation work at Eastleigh. The Cromptons usually visit Eastleigh for a classified overhaul every four years on a strictly programmed basis. However, if a locomotive has major problems within this period it may well visit the works for casual repairs. There are two categories of overhaul given to Class 33s — Intermediate and General. Both classifications entail cosmetic attention to the locomotive but interior repairs are quite different. In this view of Eastleigh main erecting shop taken on 9 August 1977 'Slim Jim' No 33207 nears completion while Class 73/1 No 73125 and Class 08 No 08028 undergo repair. *(Peter Henk)*
Pentax SP1000 55mm Takumar
Kodachrome 64 1/2 sec, f5.6

Opposite:
A large amount of stone quarrying is carried out in the Mendip Hills, North Somerset. Two branch lines serve these quarries — one from Frome to Whatley and the other to Merehead from Witham Junction. Services over the Merehead line are usually confined to Class 37, 47 and 56-hauled trains but those to Whatley can occasionally produce a pair of Class 33s. This splendid view shows Class 33 Nos 33001 and 33105, the latter still carrying the white cab windows, pulling out of Great Elm Tunnel near Whatley bound for Westbury on 19 May 1983. *(Michael Mensing)*
Bronica S2A 75mm
Nikkor
Agfa R100S 1/600, f5

Left. The Cliffe and Grain freight-only branches that diverge from the Eastern Section main line at Hoo Junction see a sizeable amount of freight and oil traffic. Most of the freight consists of aggregate services operating from Cliffe Brett Marine, carrying stone to discharge terminals at Stewarts Lane, Park Royal, Angerstein Wharf and Purley. Trains are usually formed of block formations of 71 ton-capacity bogie hoppers which are roof-loaded and floor-discharged. The crew of narrow profile Crompton No 33202 climb aboard at the Cliffe Brett Marine Terminal while the yard workforce take a break between loadings on 11 July 1983. *(Rodney A Lissenden)*
Pentax 6 × 7
150mm Takumar
Agfa CT18 1/125, f8

Left. With the introduction of th
Speedlink wagonload freight
service under the Railfreight
sector, a number of timetabled
air-braked freights have
commenced operation in recent
years, linking all areas together a
an air brake network (ABN) to
take customers' goods from
private sidings one day and delive
it to the consumer the next.
Dover, with its sizeable dock
complex, generates a substantia
amount of traffic for the ABN an
several Speedlink trains operate
daily. The 1635 Dover-Bescot
ABS, formed entirely of
Continental stock, departs from
Sandling Tunnel and heads
towards Westenhanger on 27
April 1984 headed by HG-
allocated No 33059.
(Rodney A Lissenden)
Pentax 6 × 7 150mm Takumar
Agfa CT18 1/500, f4

Right. The only timetabled
requirement today for a slim-li
Crompton is the Mondays-
excepted 1130 Mountfield
Sidings-Northfleet gypsum trai
and the 1458 return. The train
formed of scaled down MGR-
type wagons and operated on t
block train principle. Gypsum
mined at Mountfield, which is r
connected by a short branch o
the Tonbridge-Hastings line ne
Battle, and is used at Northfleet
the production of powdered
cement. The 1130 from
Mountfield is pictured pulling
away from Etchingham on 18
February 1985 after a light
sprinkling of snow, motive pow
on this occasion being provided
No 33212 — the last Crompton
be built, entering service in M
1962. *(Rodney A Lissenden)*
Pentax 6 × 7 150mm Takuma
Ektachrome 200 1/500, f8

Warning
Do not trespass
on the Railway
Penalty £200

Beware
of trains

Above. Diverging off the non-electrified Ash-ford-Hastings line at Appledore is the 9½-mile single track branch to Lydd Town and Dungeness. Today no timetabled traffic traverses the branch and the only train to use it is the infrequent nuclear flask traffic operating between the Windscale nuclear reprocessing plant and the CEGB nuclear power station at Dungeness. The train is usually formed of a XKB type flask wagon sandwiched between two barrier vehicles, with a goods brake at the rear. The train operated on 25 August 1983 and headed by No 33206 is seen in this study taken near Appledore. *(Paul D Shannon)*
Olympus OM1 50mm Zuiko Kodachrome 64 1/250, f5.6-8

Right. The Coastway branch from Lewes to Seaford sees only occasional locomotive-hauled freight to Newhaven and this is nor-mally formed of automotive or stone traffic. There are facilities at Newhaven Marine for the handling of Freightliner traffic if necessary, and on rare occasions these have been put to use, but only when other coastal terminals such as those at Southampton, Tilbury and Felix-stowe have been out of action. Class 33/0 No 33060 shunts at Newhaven Town on 26 August 1983 with a short colourful Freight-liner set. *(Paul D Shannon)*
Olympus OM1 50mm Zuiko Kodachrome 64 1/250, f5.6-8

The privately-owned
Venice Simplon Orient
Express (VSOE) entered
service in the summer of
1982, offering luxurious
service between London
Victoria and Venice. Due to
operating differences it was
not possible to take the
complete train through to
Venice, so two trains were
purchased by the train's
operators, Sea Containers
Ltd, one to be used in
England and the other on
the Continent. The British
train formed of Pullman
vehicles commenced
working two return trips
per week between London
and Folkestone Harbour,
spending the remainder of
its time stabled at Stewarts
Lane. These dormant
periods were financially
unsuitable for the owners
and soon revised services
were introduced. The
VSOE is usually operated
on its Folkestone Harbour
duties by Class 73s but
when this illustration was
taken on 26 August 1984
narrow-bodied Class 33/2
No 33205 was used to haul
the train from Folkestone
Harbour to Folkestone
East, and is seen under full
power lifting the set away
from the Harbour station.
(Mike Pope)
Agfa R100S

It soon became apparent to the VSOE operators that if their luxurious train was made available to the charter market at a realistic cost, substantial additional revenue could be raised. By 1984 the train could be found on the main lines of Britain at least once a week visiting such locations as Brockenhurst, Bristol, York, Oxford, Paignton and many other destinations. As the train is stationed at Stewarts Lane an SR diesel is usually diagrammed for at least part of its journey, this sometimes taking SR motive power to 'foreign' locations. On 24 November 1984 the set was chartered by a group of wealthy racegoers to take them from Victoria to Newbury Racecourse. Motive power was provided by HG-allocated No 33056 *The Burma Star*, seen here near Aldermaston. *(Ken Harris)*
Pentax SP1000   55mm Takumar
Kodachrome 64   1/500, f4

The last rays of evening sun highlight the track and trains at Basingstoke on 29 September 1984, the train arriving behind No 33014 being a diverted Portsmouth Harbour-Bristol service running via Basingstoke and Andover due to engineering work in the Southampton area. A trio of all three Class 33 variants is completed by Nos 33203 and 33105, the last to retain white cab window surrounds, stabled on the right awaiting their turns to take over rerouted services. *(Ken Harris)*
Yashica TL Electro X 135mm Vivitar Kodachrome 64 1/500, f4